ANTIGONE IN SPRING

ALSO BY NATHALIE BOISVERT

ANTIGONE IN SPRING

A PLAY

NATHALIE BOISVERT

TRANSLATED FROM THE FRENCH
BY HUGH HAZELTON

WITH A FOREWORD BY CHANTAL BILODEAU

TALONBOOKS

Talonbooks
9259 Shaughnessy Street, Vancouver, British Columbia, Canada v6p 6r4
talonbooks.com

Talonbooks is located on xʷməθkʷəy̓əm, Sḵwx̱wú7mesh, and səlilwətaɬ Lands.

First printing: 2023

Typeset in Minion
Printed and bound in Canada on 100% post-consumer recycled paper

Cover illustration, interior and cover design by Leslie Smith

Talonbooks acknowledges the financial support of the Canada Council for the Arts, the Government of Canada through the Canada Book Fund, and the Province of British Columbia through the British Columbia Arts Council and the Book Publishing Tax Credit.

This work was originally published in French as *Antigone au printemps* by Leméac Éditeur, Montréal, Québec, in 2017. We acknowledge the financial support of the Government of Canada through the National Translation Program for Book Publishing, an initiative of the *Roadmap for Canada's Official Languages 2013–2018: Education, Immigration, Communities*, for our translation activities.

Rights to produce *Antigone in Spring*, in whole or in part, in any medium by any group, amateur or professional, are retained by the author. Interested persons are requested to contact the author at www.formationnathalieboisvert.com.

Library and Archives Canada Cataloguing in Publication

Title: Antigone in spring : a play / Nathalie Boisvert ; translated by Hugh Hazelton.
Other titles: Antigone au printemps. English
Names: Boisvert, Nathalie, 1965- author. | Hazelton, Hugh, 1946- translator.
Description: Translation of: Antigone au printemps.
Identifiers: Canadiana 20230465412 | ISBN 9781772015591 (softcover)
Classification: LCC PS8553.O46787 A6613 2023 | DDC C842/.54—dc23

*Dedicated to the student protesters
of the Maple Spring in 2012*

Foreword by Chantal Bilodeau   ix

Antigone in Spring   1

Production History   2

Characters and Setting   3

Afterword: 103
     History and Translation by Hugh Hazelton

Foreword

A family learns that the bank is foreclosing on their house. A corrupt man, who secretly spreads pollutants in his fields, is paying good money to entice young men to join his army. And desperate people are taking to the streets in anger while dead birds continue to fall from the sky. Sadly, these story elements in *Antigone in Spring* could be current news headlines. While the twenty-first century gave us incredible technological advances, it has also eroded the very fabric of our societies and brought us to the brink of environmental catastrophe.

How do we talk about our interlocking crises when our collective well of energy and hope is running so low? How do we wrest power from those who abuse it and break through ideological polarization? If we want the human species to not only survive but thrive, we desperately need to heal ourselves and our planet. However, the cycle of media sensationalism keeps us trapped in a position where knee-jerk reaction is the only possible response. We need stories that engage us in different ways, stories that give us the time and space to process what is happening and choose the best course of action.

Antigone in Spring is one such story. In her reimagining of the titular character's story, Nathalie Boisvert blurs the lines between Sophocles's tragedy and today's predicaments. She shows that the nearly 2,500-year-old Greek myth is still utterly relevant. Whether families are cursed or broken, murderous rulers self-appointed or "elected," and disobeying women princesses or activists, we can recognize a world that has become all too familiar and reflect on who we are, as well as who we want to be, in it.

At the heart of the play is the recurring phrase "It's never the way you thought." All three characters – Antigone, Eteocles, and Polynices – say the words, eventually whispering them in unison. At first it is not clear what the phrase refers to. Then as the story progresses and the family unit is shattered, it seems to hint at our inability to anticipate change. Of course things change all the time; we all know that. Change is the very definition of life. Yet we can never quite guess what the nature of the change will be and prepare for it. Later in the play, the phrase points to the ultimate change in a human life: the transition from life to death.

There is something poignant about the idea that anticipating the manner of our death might somehow bring comfort. Perhaps this unknown – what our journey from life to death will look like – is part of why it is so distressing to be alive today. We talk a lot about how our lives are changing in an age of environmental destruction and crumbling democracies, but we never discuss how our deaths might be changing, too. Before 9/11, could we have imagined that outside of an armed conflict, thousands of bodies might be pulverized into nothingness in a matter of seconds? Before COVID-19, and with the means to treat and cure so many ailments, could we have imagined that millions of people of all ages and walks of life might be wiped out seemingly overnight? We live in an age of extremes. The visions we may have had of our journeying to the other side are now necessarily coloured by how these extremes have and continue to play out.

"It's never the way you thought." Uncertainty has always been part of life but over the last few centuries, we in the industrialized world have tricked ourselves into believing that we can anticipate and control most everything. We have created the illusion of lasting safety, stability, and predictability. As this illusion cracks open and the truth of our vulnerability is revealed once again, what choices will we make, collectively and individually? In the play, Antigone precipitates her own death as her only option to undermine the authoritarian regime. We, thankfully, have more options and more time before we are completely backed against the wall. May Antigone's tale remind us that now – right now – is the best time to start building the future we desire and stave off the worst.

—CHANTAL BILODEAU

Antigone in Spring

Production History

Antigone au printemps was first produced on April 4, 2017, by Le Dôme créations théâtrales at the Théâtre Denise-Pelletier in Montréal, Québec, with the following cast and crew:

ANTIGONE	Léane Labrèche-Dor
ÉTÉOCLE	Xavier Huard
POLYNICE	Frédéric Millaire-Zouvi

Director	Frédéric Sasseville-Painchaud
Assistant Director	Olivier Sylvestre
Set and Costume Designer	Xavier Mary
Lighting Designer	Chantal Labonté
Sound Designer	Mykalle Bielinski

Characters

ANTIGONE, seventeen years old
ETEOCLES and POLYNICES, in their twenties

Setting

The action takes place in a fictional Montréal, sometime
in the spring.
The stage area represents a public square, where the scenes of
the play will be presented.
The text of the play should be interpreted like a musical score.

Prologue

ANTIGONE, ETEOCLES, and POLYNICES
Rivière Éternité, July,
Oedipus and Jocasta's cottage.
It's the end of the night.
The house is quiet.
It's cool, almost cold.
There's a smell of burning wood.
Dampness.
The forest.
The first ray of sunlight breaks through the mist,
the grey light of dawn.
The first bird cries out for the first time
shyly
almost impossible to hear.
A cry that's almost human.
The others, as if it's given the signal,
the others begin to sing
all at once
like a single bird
with many voices.
A deafening racket.
Jocasta.
Jocasta and Oedipus.
Asleep.
Entwined
on the old yellow couch
with the broken springs.

Jocasta
her hair tousled
her sunglasses on the tip of her nose.
Her head resting on Oedipus's chest
as it rises and falls
with his breath.
On the floor
empty beer bottles
a full ashtray
their clothes scattered about.
They'd covered their legs
with the blanket.
Their ringless fingers entwined
clinging to each other like a last chance.
Outside
the sun is rising.
There's a smell
of spruce,
wildflowers.
The mist is rising.
The sky
the sky is pink
with blue streaks.

ANTIGONE, ETEOCLES, and
POLYNICES talk among themselves.

ANTIGONE
It's never the way you thought.

POLYNICES
No.

ANTIGONE and **ETEOCLES**
No.

ANTIGONE
(*to the audience*) The story begins just like that.
A typical family in a typical cottage.
The scent of freshly cut grass on Sunday.
The feverish whirr of a lawn mower.
The grey carpet, the furniture you sink into, lose yourself in.

ETEOCLES
At first, there's this vague memory
of a black-and-white toy car
that would start to roar when you'd roll it along
an unbearable siren that made Jocasta
my mother
start swearing
and infuriated Antigone in her highchair.

POLYNICES
(*to ANTIGONE*) Antigone,
who still can't stand noise.

ETEOCLES

(*to ANTIGONE*) Or anything else.

ANTIGONE

(*to the audience*) The story begins just like that.
In the comfort
of the smell of baseboard heaters
of bleach
of the Mr. Clean and Windex that Jocasta
would use to make the windows shine.
With the smell of a fire
as artificial as the rest
switched on by remote control.

> *ANTIGONE, ETEOCLES, and*
> *POLYNICES talk among themselves.*

POLYNICES

It's never the way you thought.

ETEOCLES

No.

ANTIGONE

No.
(*to the audience*) A man
named Laius
who Jocasta threw out
after a string of calls to 911 for spousal abuse.

POLYNICES

Then Oedipus shows up.

ANTIGONE

Too handsome, too young.

POLYNICES
The neighbours start talking.

ANTIGONE
Kids laugh.

> *ANTIGONE, ETEOCLES, and*
> *POLYNICES talk among themselves.*

ETEOCLES
Oedipus and Jocasta hide away as often as possible
in Rivière Éternité.

POLYNICES
The cottage at the end of the earth!

ANTIGONE
Every summer spent playing in the water,
dreaming, sitting in Oedipus's boat
while you'd try to catch
a pike.

POLYNICES
A salmon!

ETEOCLES
A salmon trout!

ANTIGONE
(*to POLYNICES*) You were too soft to keep the fish.

ETEOCLES
(*to POLYNICES*) You'd throw it back in the water!

ANTIGONE
I'd applaud.
I didn't like dead animals either.

POLYNICES
I still don't.

ETEOCLES
Polynices and his animals!

ANTIGONE
His birds!

POLYNICES
The blackbirds that fell out of their nest.
I would have liked so much to...

ETEOCLES
Polynices, you took yourself for a mother blackbird.
Every summer, the same story!

ANTIGONE
You'd pick up the birds that fell out of their nest
and take them to your room.

ETEOCLES
Do you remember the time Jocasta found them
with their mouths open, barely alive
in your chest of drawers!

POLYNICES
That was your fault, Eteocles!
You never could keep a secret!

ANTIGONE
She began to shriek.

ETEOCLES
An infestation!

ANTIGONE
Rats!

POLYNICES
I'd rescued three of them.
Three beautiful blackbirds
set free into the summer sky
at dawn.

ETEOCLES
Polynices the saviour!

POLYNICES
Oh shut up!

ANTIGONE
(*to the audience*) All I wanted was to watch the sky turn pink
in the white mist of morning
to breathe in the scent of your Player's Lights.

ETEOCLES
And forget about school.

POLYNICES
The other kids.

ETEOCLES
Their laughter like rocks against the back of your head.

ANTIGONE
Jocasta
the sadness in her eyes
of not being a young mother.

POLYNICES
She'd hide
in her car.

ETEOCLES
Wouldn't even go into the schoolyard.

ANTIGONE
We'd pretend not to hear them.
We'd cross it together, like soldiers in an army.

ANTIGONE, ETEOCLES, and
POLYNICES talk among themselves.

POLYNICES
I was often ashamed.
Ashamed of her, of them.
I would have liked a place
in the ranks of ordinary people
nothing special about them
nondescript.

ANTIGONE
You never told us that.

POLYNICES
It's something you don't talk about.

ETEOCLES
I always knew.
I would have liked to stay there.

ANTIGONE, ETEOCLES, and POLYNICES
Rivière Éternité.

ETEOCLES
So much.
Sitting in the boat with my fishing rod.

ANTIGONE
The smell of wild raspberry bushes.

POLYNICES
Oedipus and Jocasta's laughter in the distance.

ANTIGONE
Jocasta without her makeup
with her big glasses.

ETEOCLES
Oedipus thought she was beautiful.

POLYNICES
Like that!

ETEOCLES
The fire that Jocasta would make in the old stove
the smell of coffee.

ANTIGONE
The bread that she'd burn.

POLYNICES
Every time.

ANTIGONE
The smoke detector would go off.

POLYNICES
And jolt Oedipus awake!

ANTIGONE
He used to get up late. I was always the one who awoke him.

POLYNICES
You were his favourite.

ANTIGONE
Every morning I'd snuggle up to him. I'd make believe he was a house, a big house where nothing bad could ever happen...

Pause.

ETEOCLES
In the fall we'd have to go back.

POLYNICES
Board up the cottage windows with plywood.

ANTIGONE
We'd fill the car up to the roof!

ETEOCLES
Piled on top of each other with the baggage.

POLYNICES
We didn't want to ever go!

ANTIGONE
(*to the audience*) And then
there was
that time.
Oedipus and Jocasta were chattering, smoking with the
windows open.

POLYNICES

With the smell of the rain
of the fog, a little acrid.

ANTIGONE

Oedipus started up the car
a bit reluctantly.

ETEOCLES

The road ahead of us,
interminable.

ANTIGONE

Then there was that bird
that fell from the sky.
Dead.
Onto the windshield, just before the bend
its body smashing with a sudden bang.

ETEOCLES

Landscape that blurs
blood that spatters.

ANTIGONE

The grey becomes red
then
the rain washes it all away.

POLYNICES

Oedipus
his forehead furrowed his eyes riveted on
the horizon.
Suddenly silent.

Long pause.

ANTIGONE, POLYNICES, and **ETEOCLES**
(*to the audience*) September.

ANTIGONE
The chaos of going back to school.

ETEOCLES
The smell of the place makes you sick to your stomach.

ANTIGONE
Oedipus stops smiling.

POLYNICES
Jocasta shouts every morning to wake us all up.

ANTIGONE
Time for the dead to rise!

ETEOCLES
That used to make me laugh!

POLYNICES
New clothes. Shoes that are too tight.

ANTIGONE
The mocking concert would start up again.

ETEOCLES
Those long days spent on your butt on hard seats not
paying attention, shutting up, the teacher with her lips too
red waving her arms at the blackboard, me with my chair
tilted back against the wall, chewing on the end of my pencil
without listening, just wanting to run out in the street
and scream.

Long pause.

ANTIGONE, ETEOCLES, and
POLYNICES talk among themselves.

ANTIGONE
You were always getting into fights about nothing!

POLYNICES
You wouldn't cut your hair.

ANTIGONE
Your long black hair, you remember?

POLYNICES
You tried to charm the girls!

ANTIGONE
That never really worked.

ETEOCLES
Shut up, both of you!

POLYNICES
Jocasta ran after you with scissors.

ANTIGONE
She used to shout, "Come here you louse so I can cut off
that mop!"

POLYNICES
And you'd run away laughing.

ANTIGONE
The same kid
who wouldn't let anyone touch him.

ETEOCLES

I don't like being hugged: it makes me feel like biting.

ANTIGONE

If you could have,
Eteocles,
just once
let me take you in my arms
especially after that.

POLYNICES and ANTIGONE

After all that.

ETEOCLES

Leave me alone.
I don't want to talk about it!

POLYNICES

(*to the audience*) All that...

ANTIGONE

This story
impossible to tell with words.

Long pause.

*ANTIGONE, ETEOCLES, and
POLYNICES talk among themselves.*

ETEOCLES

There's a letter.

ANTIGONE

Let me see it.

ETEOCLES
It's addressed to all three of us.

POLYNICES
Give it here!

ETEOCLES
A letter in a fancy envelope!

ANTIGONE
There's no return address?

POLYNICES
A letter from no one?

ETEOCLES
(*to the audience*) The damned letter.

ANTIGONE
Suspicious.

ETEOCLES
Poisonous.

POLYNICES
A bomb.

ANTIGONE
A sickness.

POLYNICES
A curse.
A letter
written with a trembling hand.

ETEOCLES

The hand of an old man.

ANTIGONE

(*to herself*) I rip open the envelope with my fingernails
my two brothers grab my arms
laughing loudly...
Outside the snow falls softly.

Long pause.

POLYNICES

(*to the audience*) A letter
from the baptism registry
an unsigned letter
a carefully folded letter.

ETEOCLES

Words
words written on paper
in black ink.
I can't say them
even repeat them.

*ANTIGONE, ETEOCLES, and
POLYNICES talk among themselves.*

ANTIGONE

Jocasta married her son!

ETEOCLES

Shut up!

ANTIGONE

(*reading*) Jocasta married her son.

POLYNICES
Oedipus
is our brother?

ANTIGONE
(*to the audience*) And then the air turns grey.

ETEOCLES
Toxic.

POLYNICES
Jocasta backs up against the wall
hides in the basement.

ANTIGONE
She stops moving, like a stone.

ETEOCLES
Everyone in the house
stops breathing.

ANTIGONE
Jocasta.

POLYNICES
Her tears don't fall
they can't find their way.
Oedipus
takes off in the car.

ANTIGONE
He never comes back.

Pause.

ETEOCLES

Oedipus, my father,
your silence
your final act of cowardice.

> *ANTIGONE, ETEOCLES, and*
> *POLYNICES talk among themselves.*

ANTIGONE

It's never the way you thought, is it?

POLYNICES and ETEOCLES

No.

> *Long pause.*

ANTIGONE

(*to the audience*) Toronto.
Walking,
putting one foot in front of the other
trying not to look like I don't know where I'm going.
It's cold.
The sun is setting,
the buildings cast shadows over the sidewalks.
People hurry along.
It's windy here, you have to admit,
between these buildings.
It feels like a river
a river of wind that takes your breath away as you walk.
Night falls quickly, already you can't see the sky.
Everyone has a house, a life, warm bodies that await them,
steaming plates, the hum of the television.
They don't question anything.
They put one foot in front of the other and continue
walking on.

He told me
St. Andrew Station
at the corner of University and King.

Make believe I have a life,
make believe I'm one of them.
His silhouette
is there, right there,
leaning against the wall,
his face covered with bandages.
Oedipus, my father?
I offer him my left cheek,
he kisses me on the right.
His face.
His face is dirty.
Unshaven.
Blood on his bandages.
Blood on his cheeks.
His voice
his voice full of sand, of gravel
a voice I don't recognize.
Something raving
in his tone.
He speaks too fast or too slow.
His eyes
gouged out.

> *Something breaks within ANTIGONE.*
> *The sound of crystal shattering.*

I feel dizzy.
I'm going to be sick.
A man.
Old, ugly, who smells of urine.
His hands, his hands that were strong and smooth
his hands with the rings

that Jocasta bought him
his hands
red, dry, blue
covered with frostbite
trembling from cold, lack of alcohol.
His words: a hand on my neck
choking me.
I'm unable
to speak, to move.

He leaves
without looking at me
without turning round
in the middle
of trash flying in the wind
lost dogs, beggars hurrying along
in the frozen air of King Street
the din of cars, horns
people talking on their cellphones.
Darkness falls suddenly.
The cold of Toronto
devours my insides.

Oedipus, my father
I'll never see you again.

Long pause.

ANTIGONE returns to the house.
ANTIGONE, ETEOCLES, and
POLYNICES talk among themselves.

ANTIGONE
I'm home!

Pause.

Dead plants.
Mountains of dirty clothes, dishes.
There's no air in here, it's stifling.
Polynices, open the window!
It stinks of
rotting meat dust foul water squalor.
I feel sick to my stomach.

Pause.

What's happened here?
The house?
You two...
You've got bags under your eyes, your hair is filthy.
Jocasta?

Pause.

ETEOCLES
Gone to the sun.

POLYNICES
Can't move anymore.

ANTIGONE
When's she coming back?

ETEOCLES
I don't know.

Pause.

ETEOCLES
Yesterday, the men from the bank came by.

We didn't let them in.
They'll be back to foreclose on the house.
The last thing we have left.

ANTIGONE
The suitcases on the floor –
whose are they?

ETEOCLES
Mine.

ANTIGONE
You're going?

Pause.

Where to? Answer me!

ETEOCLES
Creon is hiring.

POLYNICES
Creon spreads pollutants on the fields
without telling people, but you, Eteocles,
you're signing up for him!

ANTIGONE
Dead birds are starting to fall from the sky.
Everywhere.

ETEOCLES
Creon pays good money!
Why don't you join too?

POLYNICES
Creon's corrupt.

ANTIGONE

Oedipus hates him.

ETEOCLES

Oedipus!
Where is he now?
All he's done is leave us on our own.
Do you forgive him?

POLYNICES

Oedipus warned us about Creon
long ago!

ETEOCLES

Oedipus never lived in the real world.
A dreamer who wasted his time writing,
talking on and on about nothing!

ANTIGONE

Creon targets young men
without hope, without work.
He breaks them in and pays them well
so they'll crack down on the crowds with tear gas and
nightsticks.

POLYNICES

Creon controls the media,
the corporations!
There are hundreds of people – workers, the unemployed,
students –
ready to rise up against him.

ETEOCLES

We'll track them down and find them, Polynices.
We're stronger than they are.
Cut the blather.

You're putting Antigone in danger,
her and all the other people you indoctrinate.

POLYNICES

Who indoctrinates whom?

ANTIGONE

Creon refuses to be merciful
the way other people turn down a coffee!

POLYNICES

His men take protesters away
to unknown places.

ANTIGONE

No one sees them for days.

POLYNICES

They come back broken,
silent.

ETEOCLES

And where will you go when Creon's men have taken
everything away?
Where to?

ANTIGONE

We'll figure out something. You won't, though, not after
all that.

ETEOCLES

When they come to clear out the house and evict you
by force,
where will you go?

POLYNICES
You're deserting us?

ETEOCLES
Shut up.

ANTIGONE
The house!
It's not important!
It's nothing!
Just bricks, plaster, and cement!
Stay!

ETEOCLES
Who's going to take care of Antigone? Who's going to pay, now that everything's collapsing?

ANTIGONE
I don't need anyone!

Pause.

ETEOCLES
Their van is waiting for me.
Let me leave.

POLYNICES
You'll regret it one day, Eteocles.

ETEOCLES
Shut up, Polynices.

POLYNICES
You'll regret it all.

ETEOCLES

Let me take my suitcase.

POLYNICES

You'll be sorry for this decision.

ETEOCLES

Get out of my way.

> *POLYNICES slowly lets ETEOCLES by.*

ANTIGONE

Eteocles, don't!

> *Pause.*

POLYNICES

(*to the audience*) The sun was out when Eteocles left.
A cold winter sun
that hurt your eyes.
Inside the house
the ticking of the clock
the noise of the refrigerator
the blare of the television
suddenly filled
the whole place.

ANTIGONE

A taste of dust in your mouth.

> *Long pause.*

ETEOCLES

(*to the audience*) A uniform, a beautiful uniform
that squares your shoulders
a uniform that turns heads

a uniform that, at last,
makes us
somebody.
The kepi
a few more inches
the boots too.
Become
I've become
me
Eteocles
a giant.
My head, shaven, my cheeks, hard, my face, immobile.
The hole
still there
but my head high
despite all that.

   Pause.

Sitting in the truck
I salute the guard
who's come to get me.
We roll on for an hour, an hour and a half,
the guard's face
expressionless
his eyes glum.
He answers yes
or no
to my questions.
The traffic is heavy
the traffic is slow
we finally arrive.
A long grey building
at the end of an industrial park
that I don't know.
I'm assigned

a locker.
A green locker where I put my things.
Next to it, there's a dormitory
the beds all the same
the beds perfectly made.
The sheets are white, the blankets grey.
On the wall, a picture of Creon.
Smiling.
Honest.
Behind him, his army at attention.
The soldiers' faces aren't visible
you can only see their legs, arms, kepis,
weapons.
"Social peace is priceless."
That's what is written at the top of the poster.
They bring me before a man
my superior
a sergeant.
Barely older than I am!
He explains to me:
You've got to say yes to everything.
Don't ask any questions
follow the rules.
Shoot when you're ordered to
follow the protocol
during arrests.
Do not show emotion.
Do not smile.
They show us how to march in order
to remain stoic when faced with pain.
They show us how to be silent.
Not to answer when spoken to.
And to answer yes
to the sergeant.
They make us run.
They make us run for nothing.

They make us crawl.
They make us start over.
A kid barely sixteen years old
cracks.
He starts to cry.
The sergeant kicks him with his boots
kicks him in the ribs.
A rib breaks:
the kid writhes with pain.
The sergeant continues.
I grit my teeth.
I feel an urge to hit the sergeant.
I clench my fists I remain silent.

Pause.

POLYNICES

It's cold, a fine dry cold of the end of fall.
You can feel the sun's caress
gliding across your skin.
No one speaks.
We're
tired.
The night
has been long
and
we're determined.
We march
towards the bridge.
The city
begins to stir
to awaken from its morning torpor.
The sun rises higher.
The hubbub of the cars
blends into the murmur of the slogans
that a few girls chant softly.

The bridge
we arrive at the bridge
then
a human mass
we lie down one upon the other
to block its access.
Sit-in in the shape of a mass grave.
There's nothing left
nothing left to lose.
The boots
the boots of Creon's soldiers
in the distance.
I have no doubt
that they'd like to kill us.
There will be blood.
They're here
they grab the weakest ones
they bludgeon them
they handcuff them.
The smoke that
chokes.
Smell of gasoline, of rot.
The helpless drivers
held hostage in their metal coffins
honk
deafening us.
The shouting of the soldiers.
They direct it towards us
to restore order to the traffic.
A girl
the girl to my left
smiles at me.
An island of warmth in
this sad morning.
She throws herself at a car to stop it.
The car stops too late.

Her body rolls
under the wheels of a four-by-four.
She gets up
her face covered with blood
with mud
defeated.
The soldiers
take her away.
Her
Argie.

I
we
standing
together
welded by
rage
the anger that
splits your guts
hurts
overwhelms.
I'm shaking my hands like claws I want
to smash
demolish
burn
destroy.

Laughter in the cry of sirens
hands full
of blood
of broken glass.

Is there anything left
at least
anything to lose?

To eradicate
them
to emasculate
them
with knives a saw an electric drill
to gauge out their eyes
hang
them by the balls
wait for their slow death
film it
for posterity.

To be nothing more than
this blood
that
rises
to
the
head.

ETEOCLES and **POLYNICES**
Something in me is breaking.

> *ETEOCLES and POLYNICES*
> *speak between each other.*

POLYNICES
I told you, Eteocles,
that you'd regret it.

ETEOCLES
Aren't you ever going to leave me in peace, Polynices?
Your eyes on me
day and night
like a torture.

Long pause.

ANTIGONE
(*to the audience*) Time. Time has passed. Slowly.

POLYNICES
Winter's finally come.

ANTIGONE
The sun that never stops rising.

POLYNICES
Eteocles is gone. Everyone, gone.
Then
there was that morning.
Antigone asleep
drugged by the TV
on the sofa.
Outside, the lights of the city on the horizon line
like a sunrise.
The newspaper in the mailbox.
The frigid wind of February seizes my body.
The sun
a slippery sun
just barely covered with snow.
My feet stumble.
Tiny black bodies.
Hard
frozen
dead.

ANTIGONE
The street is black.

ANTIGONE and POLYNICES
speak between themselves.

POLYNICES
Antigone!

ANTIGONE
Did you see the birds? There are hundreds of them! Dead.

POLYNICES
Starlings.

ANTIGONE
No one's ever seen anything like it.

POLYNICES
They keep on falling from the sky.

ANTIGONE
They're everywhere...
On the roofs
the streets
the cars.

POLYNICES
(*to the audience*) The frozen bodies of the birds
gathered up by the ton
by the stupefied
road crews.
Pushed by the thousands into a pit
in the most deafening silence.

ANTIGONE
Everywhere
the smell of rotting carcasses.
Faint at first
then stronger and stronger.

POLYNICES
The kids who don't go out to the schoolyards anymore.

ANTIGONE
People on the telephone.

POLYNICES
On the radio.

ANTIGONE
On TV.

POLYNICES
In the classrooms.

ANTIGONE
The offices.

POLYNICES
The forums.

ANTIGONE
Night in the houses.

POLYNICES
On the pillow.

ANTIGONE
In the factories.

POLYNICES
People at last on their feet.

ANTIGONE
Together.

POLYNICES

Everywhere in the street.

> *Pause. ANTIGONE and POLYNICES*
> *speak between themselves.*

ANTIGONE

Polynices, are you hurt? Let me see.

POLYNICES

It's nothing, just a bruise.
At least I was able to escape from the squadron.

ANTIGONE

The helicopters.
It's beginning again.

POLYNICES

The crowd won't bend.
Creon can't arrest all of us anyway.

ANTIGONE

He knows how to count.
Prison is expensive.

POLYNICES

People have the right to know.

ANTIGONE

(*to the audience*) The soil keeps getting darker beneath the
bodies of the birds.

ETEOCLES

And the crowd is growing larger.
With the sun advancing and the snow retreating

chaos moves in.
Creon is nervous.

ANTIGONE, ETEOCLES, and
POLYNICES talk among themselves.

POLYNICES

He'll end up giving in
and opening the files!
So the truth finally gets out and this massacre stops.

ANTIGONE

We demand explanations!

ETEOCLES

You've already had explanations.
The fireworks competitions organized every week
that draw crowds and disturb the peace.
The useless explosions.
That's what's killing the birds.
The men of science have confirmed it.
There's nothing more to say.

ANTIGONE

The fireworks!

POLYNICES

(*to the audience*) Anger, anger and fear everywhere.
People that are asking why!
The crowd is growing bigger and bigger.

ETEOCLES

And the security services, too.

ANTIGONE
The crowd, immense, despite the special law that Creon's
decreed.

ETEOCLES
No protesting
till further notice.

Long pause.

POLYNICES
With the spring, the sun.
The earth thaws
the snow melts
the warmth, the warmth seizes the earth
rises from the soil.

ETEOCLES
The scent...

ANTIGONE
The scent
everywhere
unbearable.

POLYNICES
The crowd is organizing.

ETEOCLES
It's hardening.

ANTIGONE
Why?

POLYNICES
The silence persists.

ANTIGONE
Why?

POLYNICES
Little by little, people
begin to denounce
resign.

ETEOCLES
Disobey!

ANTIGONE
Opening their mouths to speak.

ETEOCLES
To shout!

POLYNICES
To meet together.

> *ANTIGONE, ETEOCLES, and*
> *POLYNICES talk among themselves.*

ETEOCLES
The girls are all like that
thin, badly clothed
proud.
Filthy-looking.
Young.
Like my sister
Antigone.
She marches with them. I've seen her.
Sluts. Too young!
They shout their slogan nonsense!
Go take a shower, cover yourself up!
Keep moving!

Their eyes
their eyes lit up, filled with hatred
towards the system that feeds them!
Towards Creon.

ANTIGONE

Haemon. I often see his name pass by.
His photo isn't like all the others
a flattering or comical one or one too beautiful to be true.
No, Haemon, he's
always changing his image.
Every day!

POLYNICES

Argie with her blond braids.
Argie with her laugh.
Argie with the blue vein in her temple.
Argie and her birds.

ETEOCLES

Their eyes on me.
Their disgusted eyes.

POLYNICES

Argie in tears.

ETEOCLES

Her.
The little blond with glasses.
The one who films with her cellphone.

POLYNICES

Argie who tries
to resuscitate the birds.
With beer
or vinegar.

ETEOCLES
She looks at me,
spits in my direction.

ANTIGONE
Every day he puts up the photos.
Canvasses by painters that nobody knows.

ETEOCLES
I don't say a word.
I keep my mouth shut but my hands are itching.
Burning.
My blood boils.

ANTIGONE
As for me,
I don't know the painters.
In our house, there's nothing on the walls.
Just photos of vacations
photos of school.
Sunsets.
He, Haemon,
his images speak.
They make me afraid.
Not with a fear that makes you run.
No.

ANTIGONE, ETEOCLES, and
POLYNICES talk among themselves.

POLYNICES
A fear that makes you feel like walking in the dark to get the
shivers?

ANTIGONE
Yes.

ANTIGONE, ETEOCLES, and
POLYNICES each talk to themselves.

ETEOCLES

Her.
Scarcely dressed. Fifteen years old.
Full of arrogance.
Her friends around her
their torn clothes
unshaven faces.
Their eyes that devour her.
Her.

POLYNICES

Argie
her furrowed brow.
She wants to save all the animals on earth
and the earth itself.

ANTIGONE

Haemon.
I've never seen his face completely.
Just a few fragments
sometimes his mouth painted blue
sometimes his face all scribbled over.

ETEOCLES

I approach
from the back
as they taught me at the centre.
I approach.
I can smell the odour of her skin
that penetrates
every cell of my body.

ANTIGONE

I don't even know the colour of his eyes.
He always likes my poems
even if they're clumsy.

POLYNICES

Argie
worried about others and only about others
and everything that lives.

ANTIGONE

IIe's the one who wrote me first.
A long message.

POLYNICES

I can't remember anymore when we became friends.

ANTIGONE

The sweet words of Haemon
whose face I've never completely seen.

ETEOCLES

I approach.
She thinks she's
invincible.
I throw her into the alley.
The chaos
covers us.

ANTIGONE

His forehead.

POLYNICES

Her fine long hands.

ANTIGONE
The line of his jaw.

POLYNICES
Her arms too long.

ANTIGONE
His dimples, a bit childlike.

ANTIGONE, ETEOCLES, and POLYNICES
Those lips.

ANTIGONE
Hidden by his long brown hair.

ETEOCLES
I try to handcuff her
she struggles against me.

ETEOCLES and POLYNICES
The blood goes to my head.

ANTIGONE
His arms carry a placard with the word...

ETEOCLES
"Enough."

ANTIGONE
It hides his face.
His over-white arms.

POLYNICES
Her arms...

ANTIGONE
. The muscles under his skin.
His shoulders, a bit thin.
Haemon.

POLYNICES
Argie.

ETEOCLES
I twist her arm, I can feel her bones crack.
My gloved hand over her mouth.

POLYNICES
Argie and me
in the street.

ETEOCLES
Their cameras flash
my eyes are filled
with blood with hate with tears.

POLYNICES
Running with her
to gather up the dead birds with a shovel
and send them to the government!
To city hall!
To the TV stations!
To the police stations!

ETEOCLES
I hit.
I can't see anything.
I hit
on the desire the rage the sorrow.
There's blood, smoke.
My knees tremble.

She's crying
hunched up on a stair.
Handcuffed.
Smashed to tatters.
I feel sick, I can't see anything anymore.

Pause.

There's steam on my visor.

Long pause.

ANTIGONE, ETEOCLES, and
POLYNICES talk among themselves.

POLYNICES
You've got a date with Haemon?

ANTIGONE
Yes.
He told me
"I'm the one who's going to recognize you.
I know who you are.
Your face.
I like your face.
Your words that night
your words point-blank as strong as their bullets
when standing on your bench with your megaphone
you lifted up the crowd with your poem.
Your voice.
I've carried it with me ever since that night."
My voice
he knows my voice.
He told me to wait
till exactly ten o'clock.
He's going to stand by the tree

at the centre of the plaza.
I won't be able to recognize him.
He'll be masked like all the others.
He might be waylaid
by the media
provoking
a tempest in the newspapers
and the anger of his father.
His father is Creon!

POLYNICES

Creon?

ANTIGONE

He told me
"If someone takes your hand
it will be me, Haemon.
The skin of my hands
Antigone
is rough and stained.
My nails black with paint.
I don't have soft skin.
You'll know.
Only you.
Don't say anything, above all!
Don't pronounce my name!
Don't even whisper it.
Because if my father Creon finds me
he'll throw me in prison."

POLYNICES

Are you going to go?

ANTIGONE

I'd walk for miles just to see his eyes!
I can't sleep anymore.

He's driving me crazy.

Long pause.

Time passes.

ETEOCLES
(*to the audience*) They're in a row against a wall, and I've got
to make sure
that they don't speak
that they don't weep
that they don't cry out
that they don't touch one another
that they act like we tell them to act.

ANTIGONE, ETEOCLES, and
POLYNICES talk among themselves.

POLYNICES
Since when do you do what people tell you to?

ANTIGONE
Since when?

ETEOCLES
I frisk them
confiscate their phones, their purses and wallets, their
ID cards.
My helper puts it all in a box
the box is labelled and filed away on a shelf.
They don't speak.
Almost at all.
They generally keep quiet.
They don't understand what's going to happen to them.

ANTIGONE
But you, do you understand?

ETEOCLES
(*to the audience*) They haven't thought
about the consequences
of their acts.
Haven't thought
never think about it.
The youngest of them, especially the girls, are sobbing.
They sob in silence because tears are not permitted.

POLYNICES
(*to ANTIGONE and ETEOCLES*) Tears aren't allowed we
keep our calm here we keep our calm.

ETEOCLES
(*to the audience*) This one here
a really young boy.
His glasses are broken
he's bleeding a little
his shoulders twitch like he's been shaken
by someone.
His eyes
his eyes remind me
of that summer
in Rivière Éternité.
I'd found it under a rock
a brown frog with green spots.
Oedipus hadn't yet punished me.
I'd accidentally broken a window in the cottage
and Polynices had told on me
as usual.

ANTIGONE, ETEOCLES, and
POLYNICES talk among themselves.

POLYNICES

Liar.

ETEOCLES

I held a grudge against you
and I had one against Oedipus
for punishing me.
I'd run away out the window of my bedroom.
I'd smashed the screen with my fists.

ANTIGONE

You'd given me two dollars
to keep quiet about it.

ETEOCLES

(*to the audience*) The frog
I'd tied a cord around it
and bashed it
against a tree.
Its eyes while it breathed
its eyes
begging me
to stop making it suffer
but I
I was too mad.
I was in too much pain.
The hole.

> *ANTIGONE, ETEOCLES, and*
> *POLYNICES talk among themselves.*

ANTIGONE

The endless hole in your chest.

POLYNICES

That burned into you day after day after day.

ETEOCLES

That still burns in me.
My hatred for you, Polynices,
inexpressible in words.
You, the tall handsome one brilliant joyful.
And me
me just me
incapable of living...

ANTIGONE and POLYNICES

Without darkness getting in.

ETEOCLES

(*to the audience*) I grit my teeth.
Here, tears aren't permitted.
The boy who is really young raises his head,
takes the bandage I give him,
lowers his eyes, falls silent.

>   *Pause.*

In the truck that takes us to the plaza
the others speak.
Their words
like knives that you plant into flesh:
lice-covered
sluts
· idiots
cattle herd quash
quash the herd.
Quash?
Something breaks
something's going wrong
but
I remain
I grit my teeth and I remain.

Pause. ANTIGONE, ETEOCLES, and
POLYNICES talk among themselves.

ANTIGONE
It doesn't turn out as you'd imagined.

ETEOCLES
No...

POLYNICES
No... It happens first in your stomach, like a soft twinge.

ETEOCLES
You awake one morning
and you've become
someone else.

ANTIGONE
Like an urge to live crazily and childishly at the same time.

POLYNICES
Like an urge to walk outside under the bright sun rather than
go to your course.

ANTIGONE
Walk outside in the soft air
smelling the earth that's thawing.

ETEOCLES
You're amazed
at feeling nothing.

POLYNICES
To feel Argie's hand slightly trembling a bit moist
to feel her joyful voice cascade all along each of the vertebrae
in your back

to hear the nervous laughter of Antigone and Argie
splashing the still-fresh air of an April morning.
The spring
a miracle in all this grey.

ANTIGONE
To see the snow flowing along the sidewalk
the children jumping in the puddles.

POLYNICES
Antigone and Argie barefoot on the asphalt to feel...

ANTIGONE
The warmth of the sun, at last, after the interminable winter.

> *ANTIGONE, ETEOCLES, and*
> *POLYNICES talk among themselves.*

ANTIGONE
It's never the way you thought.

ETEOCLES
No.

ANTIGONE and POLYNICES
No.

POLYNICES
(*to the audience*) The crowd hasn't arrived at the meeting
place yet.

ETEOCLES
There's just a few people lounging around here and there
on the benches around the public plaza.

POLYNICES
Antigone is drawing a flower on a placard with a demand
a tiny little red flower a bit awkwardly done.
Argie puts in some eyes and a mouth
and their laughter once again
resonates like music
over the plaza, which is still empty, still silent.

ANTIGONE
Little by little
a crowd of passersby
of curious observers.

POLYNICES
A crowd of chance of desire of sun.

ETEOCLES
A few bottles hidden in paper bags.

ANTIGONE
An indistinct murmur.

POLYNICES
Drums.

ANTIGONE
Slogans.

POLYNICES
A murmur of swallowed anger that grows
that threatens to explode, exacerbated
by the smoke from joints that circulate.

ANTIGONE and **POLYNICES**
It's never the way you thought.

ANTIGONE, ETEOCLES, and **POLYNICES**
No.

Pause.

POLYNICES
Everything happened so fast.
Eteocles and I.
Alone.
Our eyes locked on each other
our eyes welded by an anger
impossible to name.

ETEOCLES and POLYNICES
speak between each other.

ETEOCLES
Get out of here.

POLYNICES
No.

ETEOCLES
You've got no business being here.
They don't have any business here
either.
You're useless.
Go back to your classes.
Stop wasting our mother's money
and dragging Antigone into your craziness.

ANTIGONE
Nobody's dragging me anywhere.

POLYNICES
Our mother!

She's killing herself with margaritas.
She'll never come back.
Take off that idiotic
helmet.
Come with us!

ETEOCLES

Who's going to pay for you, for Antigone
when you'll have spent what's left
what's left to us
and it's gone up in smoke?

ANTIGONE

(*to the audience*) Eteocles and Polynices
years of accumulated rage in their hearts
throw themselves one onto the other.
Their bodies roll across the dirt
and they hammer each other
with their bare fists.
Eteocles's helmet rolls into the crowd.
The blood from his lip
forms a stream then a lake
on the asphalt
the asphalt where we'd been warming our feet.
Argie screams
as loud as she can.

POLYNICES

Everything happened so fast.

ETEOCLES

Suddenly...

ANTIGONE

From out of the crowd...

ETEOCLES
A gunshot.

POLYNICES
Just one.

ANTIGONE
Absurd
inane
impossible.

ETEOCLES and **POLYNICES**
Screams.

ANTIGONE
The sun glazes over, too strong.
Sweat runs down my temples.
Eteocles and Polynices, deaf and blind,
are fighting furiously.
Argie is still screaming.
I don't know what to do
I scan the horizon.
Coming towards me...

ETEOCLES and **POLYNICES**
Towards us...

ANTIGONE
Towards them...

ETEOCLES and **POLYNICES**
Three tight rows.

POLYNICES
Police from the special squadron.

ETEOCLES

Police trained for the task
in the grey buildings of the government.

ANTIGONE

They march slowly
shoulder to shoulder
thigh against thigh
emotionless
blindly
they march calmly
towards the crowd
and the crowd
rushes towards me.

ETEOCLES and **POLYNICES**

Towards us.

ANTIGONE

Towards the slower and slower bodies
of Eteocles and Polynices
who roll one over the other in their own blood
exhausted
Argie collapsed next to them crying out for them to stop.

ETEOCLES

The squad charges.

POLYNICES

The crowd flees.

ETEOCLES

A nervous animal.

POLYNICES

A horse bolting.

ANTIGONE
Quickly, too quickly
the crowd marches towards me
against me.

ETEOCLES and **POLYNICES**
Against us.

ANTIGONE
Against them.
My brothers.
My brothers grasping onto one another
in an impossible embrace.

ETEOCLES
Death wish.

POLYNICES
Rage.

ANTIGONE
Love.

ETEOCLES and **POLYNICES**
Everything blurs together.

ANTIGONE
Eteocles's blood, Polynices's tears.
Their bodies
shaking with sobs
Their bodies crushed by...

ETEOCLES
The boots...

POLYNICES

Legs that throw themselves forward…

ETEOCLES

Bodies that fall.

ANTIGONE

A hand grabs hold of mine!
Pulls at me.
A hand stained blue?

ETEOCLES and **POLYNICES**

Haemon!

ANTIGONE

I fall backwards!
I grab hold of Argie!
We're dragged behind a car
by Haemon, who's masked.
I see my brothers
disappear.
The crowd
the crowd like a mass
swallows them.
Dark with people
the plaza
is
crawling
with
people.
Piercing cries.
My body, my body wants
to throw itself
tear them away from the crowd
that's trampling them.
Haemon

his arms
suffocating me
holding me back!
Let me go, let me go!
The smoke from the bombs
my tears my cries
Argie's sobs
the suffocating smell of gasoline
blend together.
Lying under a car
I see
the human tide
pass over me
then
pull back.

Pause.

Forgotten tracks, scattered clothes
trash
masks
shoes
broken bottles.
A few girls weeping
helmets
truncheons
on the asphalt
my brothers.   ﹚
My brothers
motionless and cold
among the remains.
Dead.
Their faces pressed into each other.

POLYNICES
Amid the smoke.

ETEOCLES
The cries.

ETEOCLES and **POLYNICES**
The wails of sirens moving away.

ANTIGONE
My brothers
motionless and cold
at last united.

Pause.

POLYNICES
Argie!

ANTIGONE
Argie keeps on screaming.

ETEOCLES
The squadron around her
tightens,
like a trap.

POLYNICES
Truncheon across a child's face.

ETEOCLES
Stones, bottles, Molotov cocktails.

ANTIGONE
Haemon handcuffed
taken away forcibly by Creon's men.

ANTIGONE, ETEOCLES, and POLYNICES
The crowd
runs away
dispersed.

ETEOCLES
"We leave no one behind."

POLYNICES
As the army says.

ETEOCLES
They take hold
of my body.
They carry me away
and Polynices
as well.
My blood runs off
leaves me.
The cold.

ANTIGONE, ETEOCLES, and POLYNICES
The cold
is everywhere.

ETEOCLES
Their hands hold onto me carrying me
I'm above the crowd
the chaos.
Strong hands the gloved hands of soldiers
like talons around my calves
my legs
my neck
my arms.
A gigantic bird of prey that carries me away.

I escape
the rage
the screams...

ANTIGONE and POLYNICES
The hate.

ANTIGONE
The clamour of the crowd as it flees the sound of sirens.
The plaza deserted
except for Argie and me incapable of moving
and a few passersby at the wrong place at the wrong time.

ETEOCLES
(*to himself*) I feel nothing more.
My brother's face
his scream
his staring eyes I am he is
we are...

> ANTIGONE, ETEOCLES, and
> POLYNICES talk among themselves.

ETEOCLES and POLYNICES
Dead?

> ANTIGONE, ETEOCLES, and
> POLYNICES talk each to themselves.

ETEOCLES
I feel nothing more.
My body
put into a bag
the bag onto the metal floor
of a truck.
Antigone?

ANTIGONE
Argie's tears on my neck.
Warm.
Her hand squeezes mine
stains my fingers with blood.
Dusk falls over the plaza...

ETEOCLES
Suddenly...

POLYNICES
Cold...

ETEOCLES
And...

ANTIGONE
Empty.

> *ANTIGONE, ETEOCLES, and*
> *POLYNICES talk among themselves.*

ANTIGONE, ETEOCLES, and POLYNICES
(*whispering*) It's never the way you thought.

ANTIGONE
No.

ETEOCLES and POLYNICES
No.

> *Long pause.*

ANTIGONE
(*to herself*) The wind's come up in the deserted streets.
There isn't anyone.

Everywhere
the signs of devastation.
Broken glass, smashed placards,
huddled bodies, trembling with cold,
lying on doorsteps
forgotten.

The night
the night makes its way slowly.
How much longer
will we remain silent?

Haemon.
I imagine
his eyes
caressing me
sweetness of his breath
warm
on my closed eyes.
His lips.
The soft passage of my fingers on
his neck.
His scent
his skin, too pale,
cut grass tobacco
his hands
the rain
on my stomach.
Haemon
your hands
my hands
tremble.
Exhausted
with desire
with cold
I'm still burning.

Your eyes
behind your mask
in the photo
Haemon you
so far so far away.
The ice that's rising in the centre of my bones.
Imagining you.
Not letting go
of your hand, Haemon
just your hand in mine
your eyes that close slowly.
The cold
your arms
hold me crush me
encircle me.
I consume myself till
I disappear.
Never seen your face
just your hand in mine here
in the snow.
A thousand times imagined a thousand times reconstructed.
Alone
to end to end
never
seen
your face
never
seen
just your last painting
that
slowly
fades away.

> *Pause.*

ETEOCLES

(*to the audience*) Haemon
cut off from the world
prisoner in his own house
waits for Antigone like a miracle.
His father Creon has stationed armed guards
at the door of his bedroom, in the courtyard,
the neighbourhood.
Haemon weeps his pain
his fear
his confusion.
He lies down on the floor.
His tears flood his face.
Helpless
he crumples.
His soul leaves through the window.
It never returns.

ETEOCLES and **POLYNICES**

Everything
dims
now
in the deserted streets
of the city.

Long pause.

ANTIGONE

(*to the audience*) I've come for the bodies.
I've come
for
the
bodies.

Pause.

A man comes forward
his eyes are ringed by shadows.
He has an ugly expression.
His eyes slide over me, devour me.
I harden myself.
Your papers.
My papers?
Yes.
A card?
An identification card.
My photo taken in the winter
just before the letter
that destroyed it all.
I'd put on lipstick
like now
like today like this April morning when I no longer know
who I am.
My lipstick
is like a weapon.
I erase the sorrow, the weariness.
It's Jocasta that used to say that.
Her lipsticks.
She had dozens of them
lined up like soldiers from an army
on the counter in the bathroom.
Put on your makeup before you go out
you'll feel strong.

The man with the shadowy eyes mutters.
I don't understand anything.
This way, this way.
When he walks, his chains jingle
his keys clink together
his heels click.
Funeral music.
It's dark in here.

It smells of
hospital disinfectant
mould.
A woman is sitting at a desk
she's typing on a computer
she's typing angrily.
Her brown skirt is wrinkled
her blouse is too tight for her
she sighs
she looks at me.
Her eyes stab through me.
Knives.
The bodies? Where are the bodies?
There's only one, over here.
My heart locks on.
There's
a sheet over
the body of Eteocles
my brother.
She raises it
with a brusque
gesture.
His face
his face
his eyes
set, rigid, absent, lifeless
open
on
the night
that swallows me
in one blow.

Name?
Eteocles.
With three *E*s and one *T*: E-t-e-o-c-l-e-s.
You can move along.

But the body, the other body?
What body?
The body of Polynices.
That body, madam, is no longer there.
The body has been removed for administrative reasons.
Please head towards the exit.
We will call you.
There's no need to come back.
We'll call you.

The walls of the corridor close in on me
the sides of my throat close over my voice.
My voice no longer comes out.
My mouth pronounces thank you
without emitting a sound.
My lipstick foams.

I leave.
In the street, dead birds everywhere.
Again. Always.
The road crews are on strike.

ANTIGONE, ETEOCLES, and **POLYNICES**
It looks like
the end of the world.

ETEOCLES
They lift me up, they lay me on a table.
A man comes forward, bends over me.
Creon.
Creon's face.
Hard and closed.
He scrutinizes me.
I can see he's badly shaved.
Smell his cologne.
See the lightning in his eyes.

His hatred.
His jubilation.

They take off my clothing.
They examine me.
They wash me.
They empty me.
They sew me.
They make me up for an evening premiere.
They organize a national funeral for me.
My body clothed in a uniform.
New.
They place me in a coffin.
They turn the light on me.
There are
photos of me
everywhere.
They put flowers around me.
The nauseating smell of funeral wreaths makes
the air unbreathable.
The light always there
the wretched light on me.
It's too hot.
People by the hundreds squeeze up around me.
Journalists all worked up, they pronounce my name, they
speak...
Of a sacrifice? Sacrificed for order and social peace?
All the flowers. Dead. Like me.
Flashes from cameras.
Old women in tears, generals stinking of cigar smoke
who kneel down.
In front of me
in front of... my remains.
Outside, the noise.
Drums, smoke, gunshots crackling.
Clamour
cries.

ANTIGONE, ETEOCLES, and
POLYNICES talk among themselves.

POLYNICES
Heavily armed soldiers
take the militants against their will
handcuff them and throw them into trucks.

ETEOCLES
Like the one that brought me here.

POLYNICES
And then the spring stopped,
just like that.

Long pause.

ANTIGONE
Anyone home?
Why don't the lights work…
It's cold in here.
I've only been gone two days.
No … five.

Pause.

Five days.

Pause.

ANTIGONE lights a candle.

(*to herself*) Mud on the floor?
The cabinet doors are open.
Someone's ransacked Polynices's room!

ANTIGONE breaks down.

I can't go on anymore, I don't want to fight any longer, I don't want to walk, I don't want to cry out, I don't want to feel. The blood seems to be leaving my body, I'm not able to warm myself, I don't want to move any longer, just remain here, letting the cold take over everything.

Pause.

ANTIGONE, ETEOCLES, and
POLYNICES talk among themselves.

ETEOCLES
Antigone
you're not safe here.
You've got to leave.
Polynices is being accused of murder.
They've stretched him out on a table.
It's nighttime.
They've donned white suits
put on rubber gloves.

POLYNICES
Scalpel. They're slowly cutting open my abdomen.

ANTIGONE
They're... why?

POLYNICES
Autopsy. They want to prove that my body
doesn't show a trace of violence
and that Eteocles's body has been assaulted.
That way they'll have a free hand
to proceed
with the dismantlement of the movement

that we've created.

ETEOCLES
Creon has decreed a law
that allows the immediate arrest
of anyone suspected of having collaborated
with the movement.
He's invented
a conspiracy
created by Polynices.

ANTIGONE
A conspiracy...

POLYNICES
It's on the front page
of all the newspapers.

ANTIGONE
What?

ETEOCLES
As soon as the autopsy
is finished
and the evidence is proven.

POLYNICES
Every bit of it invented!

ETEOCLES
They'll proceed
with the arrests.

ANTIGONE
Shut up, both of you.

POLYNICES
They've put out a wanted poster
for you
they're going to interrogate you
accuse you
furnish proof that you're complicit.

ETEOCLES
Creon's men
are coming after you.
Get out of here!

ANTIGONE
No.

POLYNICES
You're giving up?

ANTIGONE
They're too strong.

POLYNICES
You can't!

ETEOCLES
Antigone!

ANTIGONE
There's nothing I can do.

Pause.

ETEOCLES
The body.

ANTIGONE
What?

ETEOCLES
Polynices's body.

POLYNICES
What?

ETEOCLES
Go get it.

ANTIGONE
No.

ETEOCLES
At the morgue.

ANTIGONE
I can't.

ETEOCLES
Make it disappear.

ANTIGONE
I don't have the strength left.

POLYNICES
Don't let them win.

ETEOCLES
Bury it.

ANTIGONE
The earth is frozen!

ETEOCLES
The river.

POLYNICES
The river's going to carry me away.

ANTIGONE
But how?
I'm all alone.

POLYNICES
Argie's still here.

Pause.

ANTIGONE
Before there was
Polynices, there, sitting on the sofa
and I, right next to him.
Eteocles nearby, enclosed in his room
with his music
and there,
there were Jocasta and Oedipus
wrapped around each other on the sofa
kissing.

The world could have fallen apart
they would have gone on smiling.

ETEOCLES
The world has fallen apart, Antigone.

Pause.

ANTIGONE
We'd always miss the bus
because of me.

I used to lose my mittens
every other day.
Polynices and Eteocles
never left without me.
How many times did we walk an hour
to get to school
our feet frozen in our winter boots
eyelashes stuck together with ice
because of me.

POLYNICES
"We never leave anyone behind."

ETEOCLES
As they say in the army...

ANTIGONE
How can I live with the image of my brothers
killed for nothing?

Long pause.

POLYNICES
(*to the audience*) Like children
like little girls
would walk across a backyard
full of dogs
Argie
Argie and Antigone...

ETEOCLES
Standing up...

POLYNICES
Walked
towards the security

guard
walked
calmly.

ANTIGONE
Holding hands
our eyes riveted on his eyes
trembling inside
we took
the spray cans of paint
in the pockets of our coats
the paint with which we'd written
a few nights before
the word
"no"
the word
"enough"
the word
"truth"
on the grey walls of government buildings
just a few nights
before this one.
Polynices still alive
his laughter his voice his smell.

When Argie's fingers
squeezed
my fingers
secret agreed-on signal
we sprayed
the guard
his eyes his mouth
sprayed
with green paint
the guard
panic-stricken
too surprised

to resist.
The guard posted there
alone
unaware
weakened exhausted
twenty years old, scarcely twenty
barely awake
at that end of night
barely able to keep on his feet
too surprised
to call for help
the guard
collapsed
wide-eyed
watched us without understanding
tear off the sheet
that covered Polynices
and take his body.

POLYNICES

Antigone and Argie
seize my body
drag it off
whatever the cost
fearing Creon's rage
his aggressiveness
his accusations.

ANTIGONE

Quick, Argie, quick!

POLYNICES

I didn't know I was so heavy
full of water, of blood, of tears.
Antigone
with her last bit of strength

pushes me onto the back seat
of Oedipus's old car.
Antigone with her face pale
closed
Antigone like a queen reigning over her own grief.
Hard.
Determined.
Antigone shouting at Argie to keep quiet
Argie who
gets out of the car
stifling
her tears with beer
and chain-smoking cigarettes.
Argie aging right before your eyes
an old lady with white hair
hunched shoulders
carrying in the hollow of her stomach
a gentle twinge
that would never leave her again.
An old woman with white hair
sitting on a bench in the plaza
motionless silent
a gentle twinge that would never leave her again.

Pause.

ETEOCLES

Antigone is alone.
Her hands white and frozen clenching the steering wheel.
Antigone
her eyes vacant
speeding ahead whatever it takes
passing cars
trucks
despite the snow
the wind.

That route
I knew it.
That snowy route went to the cottage of our childhood.

Interlude

*ANTIGONE is alone at a roadside
rest stop with her brother's body.*

ANTIGONE
(*to herself*) The cold.
The cold slowly makes its way
from the centre of my bones
to my
thorax.
A sensation of a knife that rips.

To stop myself.
To stop myself
from
thinking.
Sitting here alone in the dark with my brother's body.
Polynices frozen, his dark eyes open on the void.
All alone in a rest stop with a dead man.
The infinite in every second between two breaths.
No one
there's no one
just nature like a she-wolf ready to swallow me.

I could, here, disappear.
Nobody would ever find me
except maybe an unlikely truck driver.
He would find my body petrified next to that of my brother

the only witness to my gentle death.
He would invent a story of lovers, a false story.
We would become heroes.

ANTIGONE, ETEOCLES, and
POLYNICES talk among themselves.

ETEOCLES
That silhouette over there, look!

ANTIGONE
That building in the distance
its window broken
the light flickering.

POLYNICES
There's someone inside!

ETEOCLES
A drunken traveller who'd gone to sleep
forgotten by his companions.
He's made himself at home
in the truck stop.

POLYNICES
He's crazy, he's waiting for you.

ETEOCLES
His shadow grows as the night advances.

ANTIGONE
Wait!

POLYNICES
The door.

ETEOCLES
The door to the building
is half open ...

POLYNICES
He's going to come out and grab you!

ETEOCLES
The motor, Antigone. Quick.

ETEOCLES
(*to the audience*) The enraged militants refuse the
murder theory.
They've built an altar in memory of Polynices
and chant his innocence every night
in the smoke
the shouts
the blows.

POLYNICES
Creon's men are looking for Antigone.

ETEOCLES
They sniff out her trail like dogs.

POLYNICES
Mountains of dead birds block the streets.

ETEOCLES
The workers refuse to gather them up.

ETEOCLES and **POLYNICES**
Everything festers.

Pause.

ETEOCLES

Creon's men go back and search
through Antigone's house.
They tear out pages from the blue photo album
where Jocasta saved her memories
they find the page with "Summer '90"
Rivière Éternité
that picture of her
before
before all that
smiling
happy
with the three of us in her arms
they found
the letter.

ANTIGONE, ETEOCLES, and POLYNICES

The damned letter.

ETEOCLES

They're drawing the connections
they leave again
without even shutting the door
and throw the story
to the tabloid dogs
that take care of
finishing up the looting.

ANTIGONE

Hang onto the steering wheel
keep my eyes on the road
ignore Polynices's lifeless body
that shifts about on the back seat.
Eyes
Eteocles's eyes
appear in the rearview mirror.

His helmeted silhouette
crosses the highway.
He waves to me
the snow whirls, blinding me.
Continue
despite the urge
to stop the engine
walk into the forest
lie down like a star on the snow
and die gently
looking up at the sky
the infinite like a blanket
over my sorrow.
Charge ahead.
Don't think.

>ANTIGONE, ETEOCLES, and
>POLYNICES talk among themselves.

ETEOCLES

Creon's men are on the road
just behind you, on snowmobiles.
They're gaining on us fast
devoured by hate
obsessed enraged crazy infuriated
gusts of snow falling on their visors.

ANTIGONE

(*to herself*) The big hill.
The spruce forest.
The dead tree, struck by lightning.
The cottage, over there, on the left!
The river!
The broad blue river.
It's here.
Creon's men...

The noise I hear in the distance
I'm not dreaming.
Faster!

POLYNICES

(*to the audience*) The men are speeding at full throttle
the snow blinds them
the black road blends into the sky.

ETEOCLES

They're swearing at Antigone.

POLYNICES

Howling her name at the universe.

ETEOCLES

The universe falls silent.

POLYNICES

The river.
The dilapidated cottage nestled beneath the trees.
Antigone is sobbing dragging my body along.

ETEOCLES

Her hands are red.
They're bleeding
flayed by the cold and the effort.

POLYNICES

Antigone
alone in the middle of the woods
standing at the river's edge
looks at my frozen body.
She asks herself...

ANTIGONE

(*to herself*) How can I live after this voyage?

ETEOCLES

(*to the audience*) They lay my body in a drawer.
Fire consumes me, I turn to ashes
white ashes
ashes closed up in a vase
a vase put into a coffin.
No one cries.

POLYNICES

Creon's men are there, close
to Antigone and the river.
Antigone collapses
before the raging torrent.

ETEOCLES

Her body clutching onto Polynices.

ANTIGONE

(*to herself*) Rivière Éternité. At last.

Long pause.

POLYNICES

(*to the audience*) Creon's men running through the snow.

ANTIGONE

(*to herself*) They're coming ...
If they find me
they'll interrogate me
make me say
what they want.
Creon's power will then be endless.

ETEOCLES

(*to the audience*) Laws protecting public order.
Dismantling the network.
Random arrests.

ANTIGONE

And then
they'll have won.
And the soil will continue to darken
beneath the poisoned bodies of birds.
And we'll have marched, shouted, loved, sung
under the April sun
danced in the streets and kept watch through the nights
for nothing.
And they will, yes, they will have taken everything.
and I, I shall have lost.

Pause.

(*to herself*) Polynices, my brother
I lay you down here
in the icy bed of the river.
The cold will not harm you any longer
the cold will not harm you any longer.
Swim like before
before all this
the smoke the cries
that letter
swim like that summer back then
Polynices.

ANTIGONE, ETEOCLES, and
POLYNICES *talk among themselves.*

POLYNICES

That time when we crossed the river?

ANTIGONE
Eteocles, you, and I.

ETEOCLES
Jocasta had punished us.

POLYNICES
Oedipus was so furious.

ANTIGONE
Swim, Polynices,
they'll never find you
you know the secret currents
the whirlpools
the river's traps...

ETEOCLES
(*to the audience*) A gunshot!
Creon's men!
Footsteps
footsteps muffled by the snow.

POLYNICES
Three shadows loom up near the river
advancing rapidly on Antigone as she weeps.

ANTIGONE, ETEOCLES, and
POLYNICES talk among themselves.

ANTIGONE
Polynices, do you remember...

POLYNICES
Run!

ETEOCLES

Get out of here!

ANTIGONE

Beneath the water, Polynices,
not far from the dock
the rowboat must still be there.
We sank it once.
See if it's still there.

ETEOCLES

She has nowhere to go, Polynices.

POLYNICES

I know.

ANTIGONE

The cold
Polynices
the cold
has taken over
everywhere.
I can't go on.

POLYNICES

(*to the audience*) A second shot
like a shooting star
streaks across the darkness
without hitting Antigone.

ANTIGONE

I plunge
under the ice
the moonlight
falls on my brother who swims
who plays in the water

smiling.
I plunge in
with
my only baggage
the cascading laughter
of Eteocles and Polynices
the intertwined silhouettes of Jocasta and Oedipus
and the sweet smell of burned bread.
I dive.

ETEOCLES

Three black silhouettes
fling themselves into the river
without being able to fish out
the lifeless bodies
of Antigone and Polynices.
Rivière Éternité
full of the lost laughter of childhood
carries them away.

ANTIGONE

(*to herself*) Polynices?
I grasp your hand
you pull me
sun and far-off laughter.
I am whole.
Intact.

POLYNICES

(*to the audience*) The flayed hands of Antigone have left
red marks
on the hard white ice of the riverbank.

> *Pause.*

Creon's men stand

watching the black water as it swirls
Antigone's small black boots
gnawed by calcium
left there in the snow
as witnesses
to the tragedy
that has taken place
here
at Rivière Éternité.
And the snow and the wind have suddenly
ceased.

ETEOCLES

As if the entire universe
had broken in two.

Epilogue

ANTIGONE, ETEOCLES, and
POLYNICES, whispering alternately and
in disorder, speak to the audience.

ANTIGONE, ETEOCLES, and POLYNICES
The sun...
The sun rises.
The scent
of spruce trees.
Cut grass.
The mist rises.
The sky is pink
with blue stripes.
We walk softly
very softly
so as not to make a single plank of wood crack
the third plank in front of the door
the one with the eye inside.
Antigone was afraid of that plank
when she was little.
She thought a witch lived inside.
We walk softly
in single file.
Eteocles first
Antigone second
Polynices bringing up the rear.
As usual.
The door.
The most difficult thing

is to open the door
without being heard.
Antigone knows how to do it.
A real little spy.
She opens it so gently
as if she commanded silence.
Even the birds fall silent.
You're exaggerating.
I swear.
Outside
the scent of the awakening earth
goes to our heads.
The idea
the idea
is to jump into the river
in our pyjamas.
The river's water is warm these days...
The heatwave.
From the star Canis.
That means "dog."

Even the mosquitoes are slow
it's so hot.
Jump into the river in our pyjamas
before Jocasta catches us
and swears all the swear words on earth
naming all the saints in heaven
and shouts our names one after the other mixing them up.
Our names that the echo will shout in turn
with our laughter at the top of our lungs filling up the sky
to make the silence explode
and destroy the holy peace!
Jocasta
cranky, Jocasta, in the morning.
She always needs three coffees

or even four to get going!
That's why we like
to make her curse so much.

Jump into the river!
And stay there
on our backs
with our clothes wet
our hair around our heads like algae
our hands gripping one another
our eyes staring into the sky
the beautiful new sky that has just come up
to stay there without ever coming back
stay there floating
as if we no longer had bodies
in the water too warm
for the month of July
the water like arms that would carry us
as if we no longer had bodies
the water of Rivière Éternité
eternity
eternity
eternity.

Afterword: History and Translation

The first time I heard *Antigone in Spring*, I realized what a unique and powerful play it is. I had known Nathalie Boisvert for several years, after meeting her (and Chantal Bilodeau) at the Banff International Literary Translation Centre residency. Over time, I got to know some of her work and realized how innovative and ingenious her plays and poetry could be. She had invited friends to listen to a private reading of the play with her as Antigone, and as those three strong spectral voices began to narrate the tale of the children of Oedipus and Jocasta in a future authoritarian Québec, it all fit marvellously.

Boisvert has written twelve plays, each of which deals with the relations between individuals and society in a particular way and form of linguistic expression, experimenting with new innovations every time. All of her plays are dialogues or monologues, in which action and movement are also possible. *Antigone in Spring* is one of two plays that use narration as well as conversation among multiple characters. Few playwrights have written work that is purely acted out in words, but this technique draws the characters into closer contact with one another and brings out their differences more clearly, especially when they compare their recollections of the past, since one description can be challenged by the others. The language and accent of the characters vary according to their age, environment, or culture. *Martian Summer*, for instance, consists entirely of a dialogue between two preteen boys somewhere in Québec talking as they wait in the night for Martians to land on a hill behind them and whisk them away to outer space, far from their lives of poverty and boredom. They speak in their own form of *joual*, to the point that a short glossary was included when it was published in Belgium. Her latest play, *Facelift*, a monologue on the internet, ostensibly is about the relationship between women and their faces, giving useful tips to improve makeup for aging women, punctuated by sombre warnings about side effects and discourses on the stages of aging, as well as on the criteria of beauty in consumer society. In *Antigone in Spring*, the three young offspring of their missing parents narrate the play's events rather than physically perform them, sometimes speaking alone or with only one of the others, and other times talking together, much like a Greek chorus. Boisvert has dedicated her play to the student protesters of the 2012 Maple Spring, who demonstrated against increased university fees and demanded greater support for education and other progressive programs, and who clashed with police almost daily in the streets of Montréal.

Antigone in Spring is based on Sophocles's play *Antigone*, which was written in or before 441 BCE. It is the last of a triad of Theban plays (though it was the first written), following *Oedipus Rex* and *Oedipus at Colonus*, and focuses on Antigone's strength and courage and her loyalty to her tragic immediate family. Oedipus, her father, had been king, but after the revelation that he had killed his father and married Jocasta, his mother, he blinded himself so as never again to see his children and became a wandering beggar. His two sons were to share power, but Eteocles, the younger brother, claimed the throne for himself and exiled his older brother Polynices, who then gathered an army from outside of Thebes and went to war against him. The two brothers finally killed each other in battle, and Creon, Jocasta's brother, became king. In *Antigone*, Creon gives Eteocles a royal funeral, but forbids burial of any of the enemy, under threat of death, which leaves their bodies to be devoured by dogs and carrion birds and angers the gods. Antigone, who is engaged to Creon's son Haemon, bravely goes out night after night to spread earth over Polynices's body, for the unburied dead are believed to wander the world for eternity without attaining true afterlife. She is finally caught, and Creon declares that she must be buried alive. She manages to hang herself within her grave, after which Haemon and his mother also take their lives. The headstrong Creon has overreached his power: his vindictiveness has caused pointless chaos and suffering, and he must now bear his punishment from above.

Boisvert has said that she was greatly moved by Jean Anouilh's 1944 version of the play, which the French public interpreted as a blow against the Vichy government and Nazi occupation. In its first production in Paris, the decor and costumes were modern and the guards wore long waxed black coats, similar to those of the Gestapo. Like the original version, it has eight characters and a chorus and takes place after the brothers' demise. However, Anouilh's version centres on Antigone's visceral rejection of authoritarianism and her disgust with a corrupt, hypocritical society. The basic events in the play are the same as in the original, but the interpretation is much more psychological. After she is captured by guards stationed on the battlefield to carry out Creon's orders – and who spend their time complaining about their pay scales and difficulty in advancing in rank, completely indifferent to the dead bodies and Antigone's suffering – she is brought to Creon's office. At first, he is surprised and speaks gently to her as his niece, offering to release her if she refrains from trying to bury her brother and reintegrates into the family. She is intractable, however, and maintains that she will keep trying to bury Polynices no matter what and has accepted that she will die for it. She realizes that she has always been a rebel, never satisfied with those around her, uninterested in frills and niceties, thinner and darker than her sister, despising those who give in to orders, and maintains that everything she is doing is based on the unwritten laws of the gods. The two then engage in a fierce conversation, in which Creon reminds her that the government must go on and encourages her to drop her obstinance and accept the inequities and tragedies of the world so that life may continue and she can marry Haemon. He belittles her as an incapable and childish young woman, mocking her as she repudiates the deception and cowardice of the State, and finally tells her that he will fulfill her wish to die and sentences her to be buried alive. Moaning is later heard from her grave. Creon recognizes his son's voice and orders the grave to be uncovered, discovering that Antigone has hanged herself and Haemon has crawled in beside her and lies weeping with her in his arms. Haemon emerges from the grave, spits into his father's face, and stabs himself with his sword, after which the chorus arrives to announce that Eurydice, the queen, has slit her throat and died. The chorus surmises that Creon will now be waiting out his own death in the empty palace.

Antigone in Spring has only three characters, Antigone and her two brothers, who are now at last able to speak about their own lives. The play is set in a future Québec, where young people are protesting against Creon's dictatorship, which crushes their progressive ideas and ignores the decay of the natural world, augured by flocks of birds that fall out of the sky. Lighting and shadow are integral parts of the production, especially as characters speak. The play consists of the siblings' conversations and narrations and there is no physical action, much as in ancient Greek plays. The three begin by joyfully comparing their recollections of the tranquil summers spent at the family's cottage on the banks of Rivière Éternité. Later, back in the city, they receive a letter informing them that their father has married his mother, after which Jocasta disappears somewhere to the south, and Oedipus ends up eyeless, homeless, and covered with frostbite in Toronto. Antigone loves both her brothers, who are all that's left of the family, and tries in every way to keep them together. However, Eteocles has entered the army, and Polynices is dedicated to the overthrow of the regime; the brothers' inevitable fate is to die in combat with their arms locked around each other during a particularly violent clash between the protesters and troops. Creon is simply an implacable tyrant, with no family ties to the siblings, though Antigone is in love with Creon's son Haemon, who has joined the protesters and dies at the hands of his father's soldiers. The axis of the play is the force of youth's altruism and overwhelming desire for social justice, despite the odds, as well as the siblings' mutual love and protection.

Though it's now 2,500 years after the original play, Boisvert has bonded with it in two important ways. Firstly, by writing the entire play in verbal interaction, she is able to open the stage to conversations, arguments, and daily issues from all three speakers, or to concentrate on soliloquies, like that of Eteocles as he enters Creon's army and later describes his own funeral, or on dialogues among them. At other times, the three double as a chorus, which reinforces their relationship and reflects their actions. The printed edition is without scene or act numbers, using only an occasional half-blank page to set episodes apart. Secondly, Boisvert has chosen to write in free verse, the main poetic form of our time, which adds new power and many more linguistic options and connects with the ancient Greek custom of writing plays in poetry. Now words can be isolated or pronounced in groups, so that each verbal exchange has its own independence and resonance, and anguish and haste can be shown by eliminating punctuation. As a translator, I followed Boisvert's verbal structure carefully, within the bounds of fluent English. She has chosen a relaxed but often solemn style of language, clear and straightforward. The majority of plays composed between the time of Ancient Greece and the Renaissance were written in poetry, and most playwrights were poets themselves. There were rules as to how long lines could be, and fixed patterns of rhythm, especially as to accented syllables. French and Spanish theatre included patterns of rhyme at the end of each line; however, since English uses alliteration and assonance more than end rhyme, Shakespeare and other British playwrights of his time wrote in iambic pentameter, which was considered a natural rhythm of the English language. Starting in the late eighteenth century, however, plays began to be written in prose, which seemed to be more in tune with daily life. Few playwrights have written in poetry since 1900, and Boisvert herself has chosen free verse for this play alone. It fits the dignity of the family's tragedy without impeding the joy that they once knew.

And then there is the question of who these three beings really are. They speak continually, even after they have died, with the voices of Polynices and Eteocles constantly encouraging Antigone as she flees back to the river of their childhood with Polynices's body. They are spirits of themselves, and Antigone joins them after drowning. They speak as a single chorus in the epilogue, when all three have returned to Rivière Éternité, chanting the river's name as their voices fade away into the afterlife.

—HUGH HAZELTON

Hugh Hazelton is a writer and translator who specializes in poetry from Québec and Latin America. His translation of *Vétiver*, by Joël Des Rosiers, won the Governor General's Award for Translation in 2006. He was awarded the Linda Gaboriau Award for Translation in 2016 and the Prix Lèvres urbaines for his dedication to the advancement of poetry in 2018. He is a professor emeritus in Classics, Modern Languages, and Linguistics at Concordia University and a former co-director of the Banff International Literary Translation Centre.

Nathalie Boisvert's fifteen plays include *L'été des Martiens*, translated into both English and German and produced in Montréal, Toronto, Avignon, Brussels, Düsseldorf, and Berlin, and more recently *Facelift*, published by Éditions Somme toute. Her work has received three important awards: the 2006 Journées de Lyon des Auteurs de Théâtre for *Vie et mort d'un village*, the 2007 Prix Gratien-Gélinas for *Buffet chinois*, and the 2018 Prix Émile-Augier from the Académie française for *Antigone au printemps*, which was also a runner-up for the Governor General's Award for Drama. She lives in Dundee, Québec, where she writes, paints, gives workshops in creative writing, and organizes residencies in writing. In addition, she teaches playwriting at the École nationale de théâtre du Canada.